Citizens of
HOPE

basics of christian identity

Leader Guide

Clayton Oliphint
and
Mary Brooke Casad

Abingdon Press
Nashville

Citizens of Hope
Basics of Christian Identity
Leader Guide

CONTENTS

INTRODUCTION

You are a child of God living in a state of grace,
a full-fledged citizen of hope!

In *Citizens of Hope*, one of three studies in The Basics
series, our purpose is to help us grow as followers of Jesus
by reminding us of our true identity as people of hope.
Throughout the centuries Christians have been citizens of
hope, standing in the dark places of life and proclaiming
that God is still alive and working in the world. We, too, are
called to be citizens of hope in our world today. There are
those predicting the end of the church and those predicting
the end of the world, but as citizens of hope, we know the
story is not over. God is a God of resurrection, and God is
about the work of bringing new life to the church and the
world. Our role is to point to the God of resurrection, to
"proclaim the mighty acts of him who called [us] out of
darkness into his marvelous light" (1 Peter 2:9).

In focusing on the basics of Christian identity, group members will be reminded of their identity as beloved children of God and the difference that identity makes when confronting life's challenges. They will be challenged to adopt a hopeful perspective through the life, death, and resurrection of Jesus Christ. The study also highlights the meaning of Holy Communion by which citizens of hope are fed. And finally there is an exploration of how citizens of hope live and proclaim the resurrection faith daily, even in the midst of grief.

This four-session study is ideal for discussion groups, such as Sunday school classes and other small groups. Before the first session, each participant will need a copy of the *Citizens of Hope* participant book and should read the Introduction, How to Use This Book, and Chapter 1: Identity Crisis: Hope in Tough Times. Because not all participants will have an opportunity to read the corresponding chapters in preparation for each session, it will be important for you as the leader to summarize as you move through the discussion suggestions included in this guide. This will allow everyone to participate fully.

ABOUT THE PARTICIPANT BOOK

This study has been created especially for busy people with many demands on their time. The chapters in the participant book are short and readable, with highlighted subtitles for a quick summary of topics. At the end of each chapter, readers will find a Reflect section to record their thoughts in response to specific questions. Drawing on the imagery of a citizen of hope who is making a journey, they will be guided by the following:

⚓ *Port of Entry*

A port of entry is defined as a place where persons or goods enter a country. As Christians, our "port of entry" is Holy Scripture. This is the place from which our study and inquiry begin. Each chapter is based on a passage of Scripture, which is printed at the beginning of the chapter. The Port of Entry section invites group members to reflect further on the Scripture passage.

🖋 *Customs Declaration Form*

A customs declaration form is a statement showing goods that are being imported. Citizens must declare the goods they are bringing with them into a country, primarily because such goods may require a duty payment. This section invites group members to reflect on the insights they gained from each section of the chapter and "declare" what they've learned that was significant for them.

⚙ *Passport Stamp*

Upon entering or exiting a country, one's passport is stamped, serving as a record of the passport holder's visit. Passport stamps invoke memories of special trips. This section invites group members to share what is "stamped" on their hearts from the chapter. What was most memorable? Was it a passage of Scripture, a story, or a statement? This is an opportunity to write down the main "takeaway" from the chapter.

Encourage participants to complete each of these three items in the Reflect section of their books, explaining that this will prepare them for the group discussion.

ABOUT THIS LEADER GUIDE

This leader guide is designed to assist you in expedient planning for the group sessions. Four session guides are included, each having a suggested format of 45 to 60 minutes. Additional optional activities are provided to extend the time if needed or desired. Feel free to adapt the format and/or select activities as you wish to tailor the material for the needs of your particular group, making the study your own. You are encouraged to review the guide for each session and use the space provided to create your own plan and write notes.

Here is a brief overview of the leader prep materials and the group session guide:

Leader Prep (Before the Session)

For your preparation prior to the group session, this section includes a list of materials needed; a summary of the main idea of the session; the session goals; a biblical foundation or focus Scripture(s), along with brief commentary about the passage(s); and additional Scriptures that give further insights and support to the biblical themes of the session.

Session Guide

Welcome/Opening Prayer (5 minutes)

Welcome participants and have everyone introduce themselves if there are newcomers present. Offer a prayer of your own, or use the one provided. You also may wish to invite a group member to pray. Prayer requests may be shared at this time or at the end of the session.

Opening Activity (5 minutes)

Begin the session with an icebreaker introduction to the discussion—a question to put the group at ease and get the conversation going.

Reflect (25–40 minutes)

This portion of the session relates to the Reflect section at the end of each chapter. You will want to encourage participants to refer to each chapter's Reflect section of the book during this time as you cover the Port of Entry, Customs Declaration Form, and Passport Stamp exercises there.

⚓ *Port of Entry (5–10 minutes)*

Read the Scripture aloud and offer background information to provide context for the lesson.

✍ *Customs Declaration Form (15–25 minutes)*

This section guides you in focusing on the main insights from the chapter. Present the summary of each section of the chapter, reading the material provided or summarizing it in your own words, and then use the questions provided to lead discussion of the main points. Material for practical application is provided as well.

✪ *Passport Stamp (5 minutes)*

Next you will invite group members to share their main "take-away"—what they will remember most from this lesson.

Wrap Up (5 minutes)

Now it's time to look ahead to next week. Introduce the next chapter briefly and allow time for other announcements.

Closing Prayer (5 minutes)

Conclude the session with prayer. Offer an original prayer, praying specifically for any prayer requests, or pray the prayer provided. You also may invite one of the group members to pray or ask the group to pray the Lord's Prayer together (Matthew 6:9-13).

Extra Material for an Extended Session

Each session guide is followed by additional activities and discussion questions to give you more options in designing the session. This additional material can be used to extend discussion by 15 to 30 minutes. It also serves as a quick go-to resource if the session is running ahead of schedule and you need to fill more time.

— — — — — — — — — — — — — — —

It is our prayer that this study will bring encouragement and inspiration to all who embrace the citizenship of hope. May God bless you as you lead others to deeper faith in our Lord and Savior, Jesus Christ.

TIPS FOR FACILITATING A SMALL GROUP

- As you prepare for each session, pray for God's guidance. Pray for the participants by name—that each will receive from the study a message to deepen her or his faith as a follower of Jesus.
- Arrive at your meeting place several minutes early to prepare the room. If necessary, rearrange the chairs so participants will be comfortable and able to see each other during the discussion. Small touches such as beverages, refreshments, mints, tissue boxes, and so forth can help create an atmosphere of hospitality and welcome. Your enthusiasm for the opportunity to come together for fellowship and study will set the tone for a positive experience!
- Welcome participants as they arrive. Introduce newcomers and help them get acquainted with others.

- If appropriate, pass around pen and paper in your first session for participants to record their contact information. Seek permission of the group to send a weekly e-mail reminder about the upcoming session and prayer requests that have been shared.
- Ask participants to bring their Bibles to each session. If possible, provide extra Bibles to share with those who did not bring them.
- Make sure everyone has a copy of the book and a pen or pencil.
- Start the session on time.
- As a part of either the opening or closing prayers, invite participants to share prayer requests.
- Throughout the session, include others by inviting them to read Scripture or sections of the chapter, lead in prayer, and so forth. You can simply ask: "Would someone please read/pray?"
- Establish a climate of mutual respect and acceptance that allows each person to share honestly.
- Model openness for sharing by being willing to respond to questions first if no one else does.
- Give gentle reminders regarding time, the amount of material left to cover, and so forth to keep the conversation going forward and to discourage one person from dominating the discussion.
- Encourage everyone's participation by offering positive affirmations for responses and asking further questions to help deepen the discussion.
- At the end of the session, invite participants to the next session by noting the next chapter title.
- End the session with prayer—and end on time! Express gratitude for their attendance and participation in the discussion.

Session 1

IDENTITY CRISIS

Hope in Tough Times
Leader Prep

Materials Needed

- *Citizens of Hope* books and Bibles (participants should read Chapter 1 prior to the session)
- Pens and pencils
- Passport (optional activity)
- Board or chart paper and marker (optional activity)

Main Idea

To understand that our identity comes from God, who has claimed us as children.

Session Goals

This session is intended to help participants:

- Understand that God loves each and every one of us as a parent loves a child.
- Consider that God is with us in all circumstances, even though we may not have answers to why bad things happen in our lives and in the world.
- Recognize that God is working for good and a future with hope, even though it may not be immediately evident to us.

Biblical Foundation

¹But now thus says the LORD,
    he who created you, O Jacob,
    he who formed you, O Israel:
Do not fear, for I have redeemed you;
    I have called you by name, you are mine.
²When you pass through the waters, I will be with you;
    and through the rivers, they shall not overwhelm you;
when you walk through fire you shall not be burned,
    and the flame shall not consume you.
³For I am the LORD your God,
    the Holy One of Israel, your Savior.
I give Egypt as your ransom,
    Ethiopia and Seba in exchange for you.
⁴Because you are precious in my sight,
    and honored, and I love you,
I give people in return for you,
    nations in exchange for your life.

⁵Do not fear, for I am with you;
    I will bring your offspring from the east,
    and from the west I will gather you;
⁶I will say to the north, "Give them up,"
    and to the south, "Do not withhold;
bring my sons from far away
    and my daughters from the end of the earth—
⁷everyone who is called by my name,
    whom I created for my glory,
    whom I formed and made." . . .
¹⁹I am about to do a new thing;
    now it springs forth, do you not perceive it?
I will make a way in the wilderness
    and rivers in the desert.

                    (Isaiah 43:1-7, 19)

Isaiah was writing to people who had lost their identity and thus their hope. Their land had been overtaken, their kingdom crushed. People had been carried off into exile, and now they cried the tears of the hopeless. "How could we sing the LORD's song / in a foreign land?" (Psalm 137:4). Their religious identity was so closely tied to their land that this move away from their land had caused a real identity crisis. They had forgotten who they were and *Whose* they were.

The Lord had a word for them through the prophet Isaiah, who essentially said: "Don't be afraid. You are not forgotten. Who are you? You are mine. I know your name, even if you have forgotten it. And whatever you go through, I'll go through it with you and help you get through it. You are precious to me, and I love you." Isaiah reminded the people who God is and who they were. He appealed to them to hang on to their hope because God is a God of hope. God was with them in the midst of those tough times, and this God of hope had plans to restore them.

Additional Scriptures

> ¹*You who live in the shelter of the Most High,*
>   *who abide in the shadow of the Almighty,*
> ² *will say to the LORD, "My refuge and my fortress;*
>   *my God, in whom I trust."*
>
> (Psalm 91:1-2)

> ⁵*Trust in the LORD with all your heart,*
>   *and do not rely on your own insight.*
> ⁶*In all your ways acknowledge him,*
>   *and he will make straight your paths.*
>
> (Proverbs 3:5-6)

> ²⁸*"Come to me, all you that are weary and are carrying heavy burdens, and I will give you rest. ²⁹Take my yoke upon you, and learn from me; for I am gentle and humble in heart, and you will find rest for your souls. For my yoke is easy, and my burden is light."*
>
> (Matthew 11:28-30)

> ⁷*But we have this treasure in clay jars, so that it may be made clear that this extraordinary power belongs to God and does not come from us. ⁸We are afflicted in every way, but not crushed; perplexed, but not driven to despair; ⁹persecuted, but not forsaken; struck down, but not destroyed; ¹⁰always carrying in the body the*

16

death of Jesus, so that the life of Jesus may also be made visible in our bodies. *¹¹For while we live, we are always being given up to death for Jesus' sake, so that the life of Jesus may be made visible in our mortal flesh. ¹²So death is at work in us, but life in you.*

¹³But just as we have the same spirit of faith that is in accordance with scripture—"I believed, and so I spoke"—we also believe, and so we speak, ¹⁴because we know that the one who raised the Lord Jesus will raise us also with Jesus, and will bring us with you into his presence. ¹⁵Yes, everything is for your sake, so that grace, as it extends to more and more people, may increase thanksgiving, to the glory of God.

(2 Corinthians 4:7-15)

³Blessed be the God and Father of our Lord Jesus Christ! By his great mercy he has given us a new birth into a living hope through the resurrection of Jesus Christ from the dead, ⁴and into an inheritance that is imperishable, undefiled, and unfading, kept in heaven for you, ⁵who are being protected by the power of God through faith for a salvation ready to be revealed in the last time.

(1 Peter 1:3-5)

Session Guide

Welcome/Opening Prayer (5 minutes)

Welcome participants and make introductions, if necessary. Note that today's session is the first of a four-part series and that you will be covering the content from Chapter 1 of *Citizens of Hope.*

You may wish to begin with prayer requests to include in the opening prayer, or you may save these for the closing prayer time. Lead the group in an opening prayer, or ask a participant to pray. You may use your own prayer or the following:

Gracious God, surround us with your love and grace so that we may know you claim us as your very own, your beloved children. Amen.

Opening Activity (5 minutes)

Invite the group to share experiences they have had when traveling to a different state or country. Ask: What was it like to visit a different state from the one where you now live? How did it feel to visit a country you were not a citizen of? How did being a "stranger in a foreign land" impact your identity?

Reflect (25–40 minutes)

Read or ask a participant to read the Introduction in *Citizens of Hope* (pages 11–13). As you begin the Reflect section, review and explain the three terms you'll be exploring—Port of Entry, Customs Declaration Form, and Passport Stamp (see "How to Use This Book," pages 15–17). You will want to encourage participants to refer to the Reflect section at the end of the chapter during this time.

⚓ *Port of Entry (5–10 minutes)*

Read or ask a group member to read aloud Isaiah 43:1-7, 19, followed by the contextual background of this Scripture reading found on page 39 of *Citizens of Hope*. You may wish to share more background about this particular Scripture (see "Biblical Foundation," pages 14–15).

Ask group members to share their responses to the questions in this section:

Has there been a time when you forgot your true identity? How has God helped you understand your identity?

🖎 *Customs Declaration Form (15–25 minutes)*

Summarize each of the sections below, pausing after each summary to ask group members to share the insights they listed in their books. Discuss why the insights were significant to them, and ask how these insights can be applied in daily living.

* *You Are a Child of God*

Summary: We have an identity that has been given to us. As Christians, we have claimed that identity. That identity was given to us at our baptism. In baptism, the water symbolizes an outward and visible sign of something that is true on the inside. Our true identity is that we are children of God.

Other notes:

Discuss the following:

* What insights did you record in your books?
* Why were these insights significant to you?

- How can you apply these insights in your daily living?

- *God Is With Us*

Summary: There are things that happen to us and to people we love, and we wonder, *Why in the world do these things happen to good people?* It makes no sense to us. And perhaps the Bible never fully and satisfactorily answers that question.

But here is what the Bible does tell us: God is with us. God says, "I am with you." When you go through these things you don't understand, when you go through the tough times, when you go through the fiery trials or the raging waters, God says, "I am with you." God's answer to the question Why? is a relationship. We may not ever understand why bad things happen to good people. But this is our certainty and, therefore, our hope: God is with us!

Other notes:

Discuss the following:

- What insights did you record in your books?
- Why were these insights significant to you?
- How can you apply these insights in your daily living?

- *God Makes a Way Out of No Way*

Summary: Never doubt that, on your worst days, God is already at work preparing you for something more. God works best when things are at their worst. That's what the Resurrection tells us. When the whole world looked like it had lost its mind and crucified the Messiah, and things were at their darkest, guess what God was doing? God was already at work, raising up Jesus, preparing the world for hope.

Other notes:

Discuss the following:

- What insights did you record in your books?
- Why were these insights significant to you?
- How can you apply these insights in your daily living?

⚙ *Passport Stamp (5 minutes)*

Invite participants to share their answers to the question *What is "stamped" on your heart that you will remember most from this chapter?* Be prepared to share your own answer first if necessary to initiate discussion.

Wrap Up (5 minutes)

Ask participants to turn to Chapter 2: A Vision of Hope (*Citizens of Hope*, page 41). Say: "Our next session will focus on Romans 5:1-5," and offer any additional comments you would like to make about the focus of the next session. Let group members know that you look forward to your next time of study and prayer together. This also is a good time to communicate any announcements or group housekeeping details that need to be shared with the group.

Closing Prayer (5 minutes)

Lead the group in prayer. You may pray the prayer provided below, offer one of your own, or invite a participant to pray. If prayer requests were shared at the beginning, remind the group to include these in their daily prayer time in the coming week. Or invite prayer requests at this time and include them in the prayer. Another option is to invite everyone to recite the Lord's Prayer (Matthew 6:9-13).

Gracious and loving God, we give you thanks for this day of life. We are your children, and we are grateful for the many ways you have shown that truth to us. Forgive us when we forget our true identity as your children. We have far too often allowed the world to tell us who we are, and Lord, unfortunately we have listened and believed those voices rather than yours. Speak to our hearts today. Remind us that we belong to you, that we matter to you. No matter what obstacles we face today, help us to remember that you will be with us and already are at work preparing a way forward. Because of you and what you've done for us through Jesus Christ, we are citizens of hope. In Jesus' name. Amen.

Extra Material for an Extended Session

Extra Activities

- Bring a passport to use as a visual aid, or ask a participant to bring one. Talk about the importance of having identification documents in our world today. Ask: Like the opening story in the chapter, has anyone had an experience of losing your identification? How were you able to provide proof of your identity?

- As a group, name the privileges that come with being a citizen, listing them on a board or chart paper. Then do the same for the roles and responsibilities of a citizen. Discuss: How can both lists be applied to being a citizen of hope?

- Ask each person to make a personal list of every identity he or she claims: relationships, employment, and so forth. Discuss: How can claiming identity as a child of God impact your other identities?

- Ask participants to look up and read Scriptures included in the Additional Scriptures section. You may wish to write the list of Scriptures on a chalkboard or on individual pieces of paper to distribute.

Extra Discussion Questions

- The Bible tells us that Jesus is Emmanuel, God with us. When have you experienced God's presence in your life? How has God's presence made a difference for you?

- How has God brought hope to a hopeless situation for you? When have you seen God make a way out of no way?
- As citizens of hope, how can we best share that hope with others in our community and world?

Notes for the Session

Session 2

A VISION OF HOPE

Leader Prep

Materials Needed

- *Citizens of Hope* books and Bibles
- Pens and pencils
- Lyrics to the hymn "Be Thou My Vision" (optional activity)

Main Idea

Being citizens of hope means that we view life from the perspective of the life, death, and resurrection of Jesus Christ.

Session Goals

This session is intended to help participants:

- Consider the difference it makes to view life through the lens of Jesus' story, focusing on the life, death, and resurrection of Jesus Christ.
- Identify God as the source of hope we can rely on in all seasons of our lives.
- Recognize that even in times of suffering, we can look for signs of God's presence and activity.
- Acknowledge God's love and resurrection power that gives us renewed hope.

Biblical Foundation

¹Therefore, since we have been declared righteous by faith, we have peace with God through our Lord Jesus Christ, ²through whom we have also obtained access by faith into this grace in which we stand, and we rejoice in the hope of God's glory. ³Not only this, but we also rejoice in sufferings, knowing that suffering produces endurance, ⁴and endurance, character, and character, hope. ⁵And hope does not disappoint, because the love of God has been poured out in our hearts through the Holy Spirit who was given to us.

(Romans 5:1-5 NET)

In the first four chapters of Romans, the Apostle Paul establishes the way to be made right with God: justification. In Romans 3:21-25, he instructs that "since all have sinned and fall short of the glory of God," we are made right with God, or justified by God's grace, as a gift. This gift, which has come at the precious price of the sacrificial death of Jesus Christ on the cross, is received by faith—our trust in Who God is and what God has done.

In Romans 5:1–5, Paul begins to tell us about the fruits and benefits of this justification. Our faith in Christ gives us peace and the assurance of knowing that God's saving grace has been made accessible to all of us through Jesus Christ. God's grace gives us a foundation on which to stand and is the basis for hope in every situation. Even in our times of suffering, we can be confident that suffering is not the last word. Suffering produces endurance, and endurance produces character, and character produces hope, and hope never fails us. Even when we are suffering, God's love is being poured into our hearts through the Holy Spirit— God's way of reminding us that suffering will never be the last word.

Additional Scriptures

[16]*So we do not lose heart. Even though our outer nature is wasting away, our inner nature is being renewed day by day.* [17]*For this slight momentary affliction is preparing us for an eternal weight of glory beyond all measure,* [18]*because we look not at what can be seen but at what cannot be seen; for what can be seen is temporary, but what cannot be seen is eternal.*

[5:1] *For we know that if the earthly tent we live in is destroyed, we have a building from God, a house not made with hands, eternal in the heavens.*

(2 Corinthians 4:16–5:1)

¹⁹*Therefore, my friends, since we have confidence to enter the sanctuary by the blood of Jesus, ²⁰by the new and living way that he opened for us through the curtain (that is, through his flesh), ²¹and since we have a great priest over the house of God, ²²let us approach with a true heart in full assurance of faith, with our hearts sprinkled clean from an evil conscience and our bodies washed with pure water. ²³Let us hold fast to the confession of our hope without wavering, for he who has promised is faithful. ²⁴And let us consider how to provoke one another to love and good deeds, ²⁵not neglecting to meet together, as is the habit of some, but encouraging one another, and all the more as you see the Day approaching.*

(Hebrews 10:19-25)

¹*Then I saw a new heaven and a new earth; for the first heaven and the first earth had passed away, and the sea was no more. ²And I saw the holy city, the new Jerusalem, coming down out of heaven from God, prepared as a bride adorned for her husband. ³And I heard a loud voice from the throne saying,*

> *"See, the home of God is among mortals.*
> *He will dwell with them;*
> *they will be his peoples,*
> *and God himself will be with them;*
> *⁴he will wipe every tear from their eyes.*
> *Death will be no more;*
> *mourning and crying and pain will be no more,*
> *for the first things have passed away."*

⁵*And the one who was seated on the throne said, "See, I am making all things new." Also he said, "Write this, for these words*

are trustworthy and true." ⁶Then he said to me, "It is done! I am the Alpha and the Omega, the beginning and the end. To the thirsty I will give water as a gift from the spring of the water of life. ⁷Those who conquer will inherit these things, and I will be their God and they will be my children."

(Revelation 21:1-7)

Session Guide

Welcome/Opening Prayer (5 minutes)

Welcome participants and make introductions, if necessary. You may wish to begin with prayer requests to include in the opening prayer, or you may save these for the closing prayer time.

Lead the group in an opening prayer, or ask a participant to pray. You may use your own prayer or the one below:

O Lord, be our vision. Help us to see the world, others, and ourselves as you do. In the midst of despair, open our eyes to the possibilities of hope all around us this day, through Christ our Lord. In Jesus' name. Amen.

Opening Activity (5 minutes)

Take a poll of the group: how many wear glasses or contact lenses to improve their vision?

Ask: What would it mean for you to put on Jesus' lenses? In other words, how can you look at the situations in the world and in your life through the lens of Jesus' story?

Reflect (25–40 minutes)

You will want to encourage participants to refer to the Reflect section at the end of the chapter during this time.

⚓ *Port of Entry (5–10 minutes)*

Read or ask a group member to read Romans 5:1-5, followed by the contextual background of this Scripture reading found on page 59 of *Citizens of Hope*. You may wish to share more background about this particular Scripture (see Biblical Foundation, pages 28–31.)

Ask group members to share their responses to the questions in this section:

> Have you ever been through a "character-building" hardship and felt there was no way out? What happened? How did God help you work through that situation?

✐ *Customs Declaration Form (15–25 minutes)*

Summarize each of the sections below, pausing after each summary to ask group members to share the insights they listed in their books. Discuss why the insights were significant to them, and ask how these insights will be applied in daily living.

• *Looking Through the Right Lens*

Summary: Everyone looks at life through some type of lens. For some, it's a political lens; for others, an economic lens. There are lots of different ways we look at life. But the lens that makes the most sense for Christians is the story of Jesus. It's the story of God's love poured out for us through Jesus. When we put on the lens of the life, death, and resurrection of Jesus Christ, everything begins to grow clearer. The clarity of our vision is enhanced when we choose to look at life through that lens. We can see things in a different way than if we're just viewing life through our own personal lens.

Other notes:

Discuss the following:

- What insights did you record in your books?
- Why were these insights significant to you?
- How can you apply these insights in your daily living?

- *Source of Hope*

Summary: Hope is different than positive thinking because hope is grounded in God's love. Hope is God's gift to us. Paul tells us that we have this source of hope beyond our own ability. It's what God has done for us. God has justified us; God has made us right. It's through believing, through trusting in God, that we are made right with God and have access to this grace in which we stand. We have a ground of hope. Jesus Christ has made God's love accessible to us. In Jesus Christ, God has become close and personal to each one of us. It's in his love that we begin to see things in a new way.

Other notes:

Discuss the following:

- What insights did you record in your books?
- Why were these insights significant to you?
- How can you apply these insights in your daily living?

- *Suffering Does Not Have the Last Word*

Summary: One of the most important decisions we make in life is what we do when we suffer. When you find yourself in distress, when breaks have gone against you, when you are in a physical battle for your health or dealing with spiritual anguish, what do you do and where do you turn in those moments? That story is played out so many times in Scripture. God hears the cries of people suffering. And God offers help and hope to those who are hurting.

Other notes:

Discuss the following:

- What insights did you record in your books?
- Why were these insights significant to you?
- How can you apply these insights in your daily living?

- *Hope Never Fails Us*

Summary: A lot of things in life fail; a lot of things in life don't go right. But God's love keeps pouring into our hearts, watering our souls, trying to give us a picture of hope, trying to help us know that there is hope for us in every situation—that despair and the suffering of this world will not have the last word.

Other notes:

Discuss the following:

- What insights did you record in your books?
- Why were these insights significant to you?
- How can you apply these insights in your daily living?

⚙ *Passport Stamp (5 minutes)*

Invite participants to share their answers to the question *What is "stamped" on your heart that you will remember most from this chapter?* and tell why this was especially meaningful to them. Be prepared to share your own answer first if necessary.

Wrap Up (5 minutes)

Ask participants to turn to Chapter 3, Fed by Hope (*Citizens of Hope*, page 63). Note the title and the Reflect section for the next session. Say: "Our next session will focus on 1 Corinthians 11:23-26," and offer any additional comments you would like to make about the focus of the next session. Let group members know that you look forward to your next time of study and prayer together. This also is a good time to communicate any announcements or group housekeeping details that need to be shared with the group.

Closing Prayer (5 minutes)

Lead the group in prayer. You may pray the one provided below, offer one of your own, or invite a participant to pray. If prayer requests were shared at the beginning, remind the group to include these in their daily prayer time in the coming week. Or invite prayer requests at this time and include them in the prayer. Another option is to invite everyone to recite the Lord's Prayer (Matthew 6:9-13).

Thank you, merciful God, for offering us your strength each day and the promise of a future with hope. The story of your Son, Jesus, offers hope for the whole world and for each one of us. Help us, as citizens of that hope, to offer a word of encouragement to someone this day who is suffering. In Jesus' name. Amen.

Extra Material for an Extended Session

Extra Activities

- Invite the group to sing or recite the words to the hymn "Be Thou My Vision" (if you can't find it in your church's hymnal, you may want to search online).
- Invite the group to share stories of naturalized citizens. Perhaps there are persons in the group who are naturalized citizens or know of others who are. Ask: What was their "vision of hope" that compelled them to seek citizenship in another country?
- Ask participants to look up and read Scriptures from the Additional Scriptures section. You may wish to write the list of Scriptures on a chalkboard or on individual pieces of paper to distribute.

Extra Discussion Questions

- How does the story of Jesus offer hope to you?
- What does it mean for you to persevere and endure?
- How can you speak a word of hope to someone you know who is in need?

Notes for the Session

Session 3

FED BY HOPE

Leader Prep

Materials Needed

- *Citizens of Hope* books and Bibles
- Pens and pencils
- Elements for Holy Communion (optional activity—invite your pastor in advance to come and serve the elements at the close of the session)

Main Idea

Holy Communion is the meal by which we are spiritually nourished and fed through our connection with God and one another.

Session Goals

This session is intended to help participants:

- Understand that our relationship with Jesus becomes real to us through the life-giving food of Communion.
- Recognize that God has become intimately acquainted with our hurts, sins, and fears through the death of Jesus on the cross.
- Consider that God is not through with any of us— that he is a God of resurrection and new life.
- Claim for ourselves that God's ultimate victory is not just someday at the close of the age; God is at work today bringing about that victory.

Biblical Foundation

²³For I received from the Lord what I also handed on to you, that the Lord Jesus on the night when he was betrayed took a loaf of bread, ²⁴and when he had given thanks, he broke it and said, "This is my body that is for you. Do this in remembrance of me." ²⁵In the same way he took the cup also, after supper, saying, "This cup is the new covenant in my blood. Do this, as often as you drink it, in remembrance of me." ²⁶For as often as you eat this bread and drink the cup, you proclaim the Lord's death until he comes.

(1 Corinthians 11:23-26)

In this chapter Paul is warning the Corinthian church about abuses at the Lord's Supper. Evidently, they were partaking in the Lord's Supper in a manner that was unworthy. Some were eating or drinking too much, while others went away hungry. Those who had little were being humiliated by those who had much. The food was getting in the way of the purpose of the sacred meal of the gathered community. They seemed to have forgotten the main purpose of this sacred meal, losing their focus on why they were gathering together. (This is easy to do in a church, or any other human endeavor, for that matter. This discussion leads Paul into the importance of all members of the body of Christ in 1 Corinthians 12.)

Paul reminds the church about the actions and words of Jesus on the night of the Last Supper with his disciples: "The Lord Jesus on the night when he was betrayed took a loaf of bread, and when he had given thanks, he broke it and said, 'This is my body that is for you. Do this in remembrance of me.' In the same way he took the cup also, after supper, saying, 'This cup is the new covenant in my blood. Do this, as often as you drink it, in remembrance of me' " (vv. 23-25). Paul says that when we partake of the Lord's Supper in this way, we "proclaim the Lord's death until he comes" (v. 26). This is the holy mystery—Christ has died; Christ is risen; Christ will come again. The story is always pointing us toward hope: Christ will ultimately triumph, and his reign will be on earth as it is in heaven.

When we celebrate the Lord's Supper and remember Jesus' words, we are anticipating that future hope even as we claim the presence of Christ in our current reality.

Additional Scriptures

[14]*When the hour came, he took his place at the table, and the apostles with him.* [15]*He said to them, "I have eagerly desired to eat this Passover with you before I suffer;* [16]*for I tell you, I will not eat*

it until it is fulfilled in the kingdom of God." [17] *Then he took a cup, and after giving thanks he said, "Take this and divide it among yourselves;* [18]*for I tell you that from now on I will not drink of the fruit of the vine until the kingdom of God comes."* [19] *Then he took a loaf of bread, and when he had given thanks, he broke it and gave it to them, saying, "This is my body, which is given for you. Do this in remembrance of me."* [20] *And he did the same with the cup after supper, saying, "This cup that is poured out for you is the new covenant in my blood.* [21]*But see, the one who betrays me is with me, and his hand is on the table.* [22]*For the Son of Man is going as it has been determined, but woe to that one by whom he is betrayed!"* [23]*Then they began to ask one another which one of them it could be who would do this.*

(Luke 22:14-23)

[32]*Then Jesus said to them, "Very truly, I tell you, it was not Moses who gave you the bread from heaven, but it is my Father who gives you the true bread from heaven.* [33]*For the bread of God is that which comes down from heaven and gives life to the world."* [34]*They said to him, "Sir, give us this bread always."*

[35]*Jesus said to them, "I am the bread of life. Whoever comes to me will never be hungry, and whoever believes in me will never be thirsty.* [36]*But I said to you that you have seen me and yet do not believe.* [37]*Everything that the Father gives me will come to me, and anyone who comes to me I will never drive away;* [38]*for I have come down from heaven, not to do my own will, but the will of him who sent me.* [39]*And this is the will of him who sent me, that I should lose nothing of all that he has given me, but raise it up on the last day.* [40]*This is indeed the will of my Father, that all who see*

the Son and believe in him may have eternal life; and I will raise them up on the last day."

(John 6:32-40)

[28]As they came near the village to which they were going, he walked ahead as if he were going on. [29]But they urged him strongly, saying, "Stay with us, because it is almost evening and the day is now nearly over." So he went in to stay with them. [30]When he was at the table with them, he took bread, blessed and broke it, and gave it to them. [31]Then their eyes were opened, and they recognized him; and he vanished from their sight. [32]They said to each other, "Were not our hearts burning within us while he was talking to us on the road, while he was opening the scriptures to us?" [33]That same hour they got up and returned to Jerusalem; and they found the eleven and their companions gathered together. [34] They were saying, "The Lord has risen indeed, and he has appeared to Simon!" [35]Then they told what had happened on the road, and how he had been made known to them in the breaking of the bread.

(Luke 24:28–35)

They devoted themselves to the apostles' teaching and fellowship, to the breaking of bread and the prayers.

(Acts 2:42)

Session Guide

Welcome/Opening Prayer (5 minutes)

Welcome participants. You may wish to begin with prayer requests to include in the opening prayer, or you may save these for the closing prayer time.

Lead the group in an opening prayer, or ask a participant to pray. You may use your own prayer or the following:

Gracious and loving God, in your Son, Jesus, you offer to us the bread of life and the cup of salvation. But too often we have settled for cheap substitutes that leave us feeling empty and unsatisfied. Open us this day to the fullness of life and living that you desire for us. Help us to feast upon the hope that we find in Jesus Christ, so that we will never be hungry again. Amen.

Opening Activity (5 minutes)

If you have access to a whiteboard or large sheet of paper, list participants' responses in two columns.

Say:

One of the greatest challenges of our lives is to live in a material world but to stay grounded and fed by spiritual food. Name the ways that make you feel as though you lack something (for example: seeing what other people have, watching commercials, or seeing ads that encourage you to have something you don't have, and so on). Now, name what you *do* have that are gifts from God: family, friends, health, jobs, and so forth.

Discuss:

Can focusing on what you have instead of what you don't have change your perspective about how you are living?

Reflect (25–40 minutes total)

You will want to encourage participants to refer to the Reflect section at the end of the chapter during this time.

⚓ *Port of Entry (5–10 minutes)*

Read or ask a group member to read 1 Corinthians 11: 23-26, followed by the contextual background of this Scripture reading found on page 81 of *Citizens of Hope*. You may wish to share more background about this particular Scripture (see Biblical Foundation, pages 40–43.)

Ask group members to share their responses to the questions in this section:

> Has there been a time when receiving Holy Communion took on a special meaning for you? What made it special or gave it special meaning?

📝 *Customs Declaration Form (15–25 minutes)*

Summarize each of the sections below, pausing after each summary to ask group members to share the insights they listed in their books. Discuss why the insights were significant to them, and ask how these insights will be applied in daily living.

- *What Feeds You?*

Summary: So where do you go to be fed? Have you ever really thought about what feeds you? Where do you really find help, hope, and the strength that sustains you? We need food to stay alive. Instinctively we know this, and from our earliest moments of life we cry out for food when we are hungry. In a similar way, we have a spiritual hunger, and instinctively we know we have this need for something more. The problem is that much of what is offered to us as filling only leaves us empty.

Other notes:

Discuss the following:

- What insights did you record in your books?
- Why were these insights significant to you?
- How can you apply these insights in your daily living?

- *Something More*

Summary: Throughout the centuries, Christians have found that when they feast on the body and blood of Christ, something mystical and mysterious happens. It is in celebrating Holy Communion as a means of God's grace that we are fed in ways that nothing on this earth can do for us. We are fed with the incredible hope that we find in the holy mystery called Holy Communion.

Other notes:

Discuss the following:

- What insights did you record in your books?
- Why were these insights significant to you?

- How can you apply these insights in your daily living?

- *Christ Has Died*

Summary: As we gather around the Lord's Table and receive the body of Christ, we remember the self-sacrifice of Jesus Christ. God so loved the world that God gave his Son, and in Jesus' suffering and death, we find life and salvation from our sins. Jesus' suffering on the cross connects with our suffering in the world today. Have you ever felt alone? Have you ever experienced a situation in life when you felt hopeless, like you were abandoned? On the cross, Jesus experienced all of that and more.

Other notes:

Discuss the following:

- What insights did you record in your book?
- Why were these insights significant to you?
- How can you apply these insights in your daily living?

- *Christ Is Risen*

Summary: Each time you receive Holy Communion, remember that no matter your situation and no matter what is happening in our world today, God is a God of resurrection. As the Scriptures proclaim, the same God who raised up his Son, Jesus Christ, will raise us up also. It's God's promise. And it's not just after we die—it's here and now. God is at work resurrecting and bringing new life and hope to you and me.

Other notes:

Discuss the following:

- What insights did you record in your book?
- Why were these insights significant to you?
- How can you apply these insights in your daily living?

- *Christ Will Come Again*

Summary: The third aspect of the mystery of the Christian faith referred to in the Communion liturgy is that Christ will come again. In this Communion meal, we are pointing forward to God's ultimate victory. It is a statement of hope, reminding us that this is God's world. The God who raised his Son from the dead is not content to leave us alone and abandoned, without hope. God's promise is that this same Jesus, who died and rose again, will come in final judgment as the fulfillment of history.

Other notes:

Discuss the following:

- What insights did you record in your books?
- Why were these insights significant to you?
- How can you apply these insights in your daily living?

☼ *Passport Stamp (5 minutes)*

Invite participants to share their answers to the question *What is "stamped" on your heart that you will remember most from this chapter?* and tell why this was especially meaningful to them. Be prepared to share your own answer first if necessary.

Wrap Up (5 minutes)

Ask participants to turn to Chapter 4: Second Line Living (*Citizens of Hope*, page 87). Say: "Our next session will focus on John 20:11-18 and John 11:25-26," and offer any additional comments you would like to make about the focus of the next session. Let group members know that you look forward to your next time of study and prayer together. This also is a good time to communicate any announcements or group housekeeping details that need to be shared with the group.

Closing Prayer (5 minutes)

Lead the group in prayer. You may pray the one provided below, offer one of your own, or invite a participant to pray. If prayer requests were shared at the beginning, remind the group to include these in their daily prayer time in the coming week. Or invite prayer requests at this time and include them in the prayer. (Another option is to invite everyone to recite the Lord's Prayer, Matthew 6:9-13.)

O God, only you satisfy the hungry heart. Thank you for the gift of your grace that we experience in the body and blood of Jesus Christ. Help us day by day to be aware of the many ways you feed our souls in ways the world cannot. Send us forth to point others to this source of hope, the Bread of Life, Jesus Christ. Amen.

Extra Material for an Extended Session

Extra Activities

- Make arrangements with your pastor to close your session with the service of Holy Communion.
- Ask if anyone has assisted in serving Holy Communion before. Have them describe the experience. What was different about serving Communion rather than just receiving it?
- Ask participants to look up and read Scriptures from the Additional Scriptures section. You may wish to write the list of Scriptures on a chalkboard or on individual pieces of paper to distribute.

Extra Discussion Questions

- Have you ever bought something thinking that it would bring you happiness? What happened?
- What does Holy Communion mean to you?
- Having been fed by this spiritual food, how can you help others find the Bread of Life?

Notes for the Session

SECOND LINE LIVING

Leader Prep

Materials Needed

- *Citizens of Hope* books and Bibles
- Pens and pencils
- Lyrics for the hymn "Christ the Lord Is Risen Today" (if you can't find it in your church's hymnal, you may want to search online) (optional activity)

Main Idea

God, who has become real to us in the life, death, and resurrection of Jesus, is a God of hope and new life.

Session Goals

This session is intended to help participants:

- Claim the good news of resurrection in the midst of death.
- Recognize that keeping resurrection faith can release us from paralyzing fears.
- Consider that the despair of grief will not ultimately define our lives; our lives will be defined by the hope and love God offers to us in the risen Christ.
- Understand that in whatever we face, nothing—not even death—can separate us from God's love.

Biblical Foundation

[11]*But Mary stood weeping outside the tomb. As she wept, she bent over to look into the tomb;* [12]*and she saw two angels in white, sitting where the body of Jesus had been lying, one at the head and the other at the feet.* [13]*They said to her, "Woman, why are you weeping?" She said to them, "They have taken away my Lord, and I do not know where they have laid him."* [14]*When she had said this, she turned around and saw Jesus standing there, but she did not know that it was Jesus.* [15]*Jesus said to her, "Woman, why are you weeping? Whom are you looking for?" Supposing him to be the gardener, she said to him, "Sir, if you have carried him away, tell me where you have laid him, and I will take him away."* [16]*Jesus said to her, "Mary!" She turned and said to him in Hebrew, "Rabbouni!" (which means Teacher).* [17]*Jesus said to her, "Do not hold on to me, because I have not yet ascended to the Father. But go to my brothers and say to them, 'I am ascending to my Father and your Father, to my God and your God.'"* [18]*Mary*

Magdalene went and announced to the disciples, "I have seen the Lord"; and she told them that he had said these things to her.

(John 20:11-18)

[25]Jesus said to her, "I am the resurrection and the life. Those who believe in me, even though they die, will live, [26]and everyone who lives and believes in me will never die. Do you believe this?"

(John 11:25-26)

The Gospel of John's account of the resurrection of Jesus centers on Mary Magdalene. "Early on the first day of the week, while it was still dark..." (John 20:1). John's language speaks not only to the physical reality that the sun has not yet risen, but also to the spiritual state of Mary, whose grief is so deep she cannot see that the Son has indeed risen. Her lack of recognition is exactly what grief and other harsh realities in life do to us. But when Jesus calls her by name, Mary, once blinded by grief can now see. She goes forward to proclaim the good news, the music of the second line, telling others of the Resurrection.

In John's Gospel there are numerous "I am" statements that Jesus makes. One of those, found in John 11, captures the essence for all those who would claim to be citizens of hope: Jesus is indeed resurrection and life (v. 26). He is the source of hope and strength. Those who believe in him, indeed, shall never die. They have joined the second line chorus, proclaiming that death, as real as it is, does not have the last word. That word is the Word of God, resurrection and life, found in Jesus. We have hope in every situation because we have placed our trust in the God who raised Jesus Christ and has promised to raise us up, in life and in death also.

Additional Scriptures

¹*After the sabbath, as the first day of the week was dawning, Mary Magdalene and the other Mary went to see the tomb.* ²*And suddenly there was a great earthquake; for an angel of the Lord, descending from heaven, came and rolled back the stone and sat on it.* ³*His appearance was like lightning, and his clothing white as snow.* ⁴*For fear of him the guards shook and became like dead men.* ⁵*But the angel said to the women, "Do not be afraid; I know that you are looking for Jesus who was crucified.* ⁶*He is not here; for he has been raised, as he said. Come, see the place where he lay.* ⁷*Then go quickly and tell his disciples, 'He has been raised from the dead, and indeed he is going ahead of you to Galilee; there you will see him.' This is my message for you."* ⁸*So they left the tomb quickly with fear and great joy, and ran to tell his disciples.* ⁹*Suddenly Jesus met them and said, "Greetings!" And they came to him, took hold of his feet, and worshiped him.* ¹⁰*Then Jesus said to them, "Do not be afraid; go and tell my brothers to go to Galilee; there they will see me."*

(Matthew 28:1-10)

⁹*Now after he rose early on the first day of the week, he appeared first to Mary Magdalene, from whom he had cast out seven demons.* ¹⁰*She went out and told those who had been with him, while they were mourning and weeping.* ¹¹*But when they heard that he was alive and had been seen by her, they would not believe it.* ¹²*After this he appeared in another form to two of them, as they were walking into the country.* ¹³*And they went back and told the rest, but they did not believe them.*

(Mark 16:9-13)

¹*But on the first day of the week, at early dawn, they came to the tomb, taking the spices that they had prepared.* ²*They found the*

stone rolled away from the tomb, ³but when they went in, they did not find the body. ⁴While they were perplexed about this, suddenly two men in dazzling clothes stood beside them. ⁵The women were terrified and bowed their faces to the ground, but the men said to them, "Why do you look for the living among the dead? He is not here, but has risen. ⁶Remember how he told you, while he was still in Galilee, ⁷that the Son of Man must be handed over to sinners, and be crucified, and on the third day rise again." ⁸Then they remembered his words, ⁹and returning from the tomb, they told all this to the eleven and to all the rest. ¹⁰Now it was Mary Magdalene, Joanna, Mary the mother of James, and the other women with them who told this to the apostles. ¹¹But these words seemed to them an idle tale, and they did not believe them. ¹²But Peter got up and ran to the tomb; stooping and looking in, he saw the linen cloths by themselves; then he went home, amazed at what had happened.

(Luke 24:1-12)

³²This Jesus God raised up, and of that all of us are witnesses. ³³Being therefore exalted at the right hand of God, and having received from the Father the promise of the Holy Spirit, he has poured out this that you both see and hear. ³⁴For David did not ascend into the heavens, but he himself says,

> *'The Lord said to my Lord,*
> *"Sit at my right hand,*
> *³⁵until I make your enemies your footstool."'*

³⁶Therefore let the entire house of Israel know with certainty that God has made him both Lord and Messiah, this Jesus whom you crucified."

(Acts 2:32-36)

Session Guide

Welcome/Opening Prayer (5 minutes)

Welcome participants. You may wish to begin with prayer requests to include in the opening prayer, or you may save these for the closing prayer time.

Lead the group in an opening prayer, or ask a participant to pray. You may use your own prayer or the one below:

Living Lord, we are thankful that you dwell in our hearts. Help us know the power of your resurrection and what it can mean for us today and every day. Amen.

Opening Activity (5 minutes)

This chapter focuses on the "second line" as described on pages 87–89 in *Citizens of Hope*. Ask participants if there is a special song that symbolizes resurrection and new life for them, giving them hope when they hear it.

Reflect (25–40 minutes)

You will want to encourage participants to refer to the Reflect section at the end of the chapter during this time.

⚓ *Port of Entry (5–10 minutes)*

Read or ask a group member to read John 11:25-26 and John 20:11-18, followed by the contextual background of these Scripture readings found on page 104 of *Citizens of Hope*. You may wish to share more background about these particular Scriptures (see Biblical Foundation, pages 54–55.)

Ask group members to share their responses to the questions in this section:

Have you ever heard the risen Christ call you by name? How does the resurrection of Jesus make a difference in your life?

✍ Customs Declaration Form (15–25 minutes)

Summarize each of the sections below, pausing after each summary to ask group members to share the insights they listed in their books. Discuss why the insights were significant to them, and ask how these insights will be applied in daily living.

*   *Living the Resurrection Faith*

Summary: Resurrection changes everything. Jesus said, "I am the resurrection and life" (John 11:26). Jesus is a window into the nature of who God is. God's very nature, the ground of being in which we stand today, is the very hope of resurrection. It's at the heart of who God is: resurrection and new life.

Other notes:

Discuss the following:

- What insights did you record in your books?
- Why were these insights significant to you?
- How can you apply these insights in your daily living?

- *Faith Overcomes Fear*

Summary: Because of the second line music of resurrection, faith overcomes fear. It is our faith in God that helps us overcome our fears in life.

Other notes:

Discuss the following:

- What insights did you record in your books?
- Why were these insights significant to you?
- How can you apply these insights in your daily living?

- *Hope Outlasts Our Despair*

Summary: We know that hope is real. With God, because of the Resurrection, there are no hopeless situations, there are no hopeless people. There is no one who is beyond resurrection and redemption. There is no one beyond the reach of God to bring new life and new hope into their lives.

Other notes:

Discuss the following:

- What insights did you record in your books?
- Why were these insights significant to you?
- How can you apply these insights in your daily living?

- *Love Leaves Behind More than Death Takes Away*

Summary: We put our hope in the God of resurrection. In the midst of death, we find that God's love is more powerful. Nothing can separate us from the love of God.

Other notes:

Discuss the following:

- What insights did you record in your books?
- Why were these insights significant to you?
- How can you apply these insights in your daily living?

⚹ *Passport Stamp (5 minutes)*

Invite participants to share their answers to the question *What is "stamped" on your heart that you will remember most from this chapter?* and tell why this was especially meaningful to them. Be prepared to share your own answer first if necessary.

Wrap Up (5 minutes)

As you come to the end of this study, thank the group for their participation over these four sessions. If you will be facilitating future studies (in The Basics series or another study), invite them to be a part and note the date when the study will begin.

Closing Prayer (5 minutes)

Encourage group members to continue remembering one another and the prayer requests that have been shared in their prayers.

Lead the group in prayer. You may pray the one provided below, offer one of your own, or invite a participant to pray. If prayer requests were shared at the beginning, remind the group to include these in their daily prayer time in the coming week. Or invite prayer requests at this time and include them in the prayer. (Another option is to invite everyone to recite the Lord's Prayer, Matthew 6:9-13.)

God, you are the source of resurrection and new life. Sometimes we are overwhelmed by fear, despair, and the reality of death. Remind us again that in Jesus you have sent the second line music with the beautiful lyrics of faith, hope, and love. Help us to hear that music in the midst of our own grief, and challenge us to go out and sing the song of resurrection to those in despair. Thank you for raising up your Son, Jesus Christ. Amen.

Extra Material for an Extended Session

Extra Activities

- Sing or recite together "Christ the Lord Is Risen Today" (if you can't find it in your church's hymnal, you may want to search online).
- Invite participants to tell a story from their experience that best symbolizes the Resurrection in their lives.
- Ask participants to look up and read Scriptures from the Additional Scriptures section. You may wish to write the list of Scriptures on a chalkboard or on individual pieces of paper to distribute.

Extra Discussion Questions

- Where has your faith helped you overcome fear?
- When have you found hope in the midst of despair?
- Are there people in your community who need to hear the second line music? How might you and your faith community share second line music with others?

Notes for the Session